MW01701244

Black American Music Evolution:

The Ketu Candomblé Codes

Black American Music Evolution:

The Ketu Candomblé Codes

Jamilla Counts

(*Based on discoveries by Andrew Scott Potter*)

Note: *This book is complimented by watching this YouTube video:*
: https://m.youtube.com/watch?v=eo7NNuHGa_M&t=2497s

Copyright © 2023 Jamilla Counts

All rights reserved.

This book or any portion thereof may not be reproduced or used in any manner whatsoever without the express written permission of the publisher and author except for the use of brief quotations in a book review.

Printed in the United States of America

First Printing, 2023

ISBN13: 9781951883997

The Butterfly Typeface Publishing
PO Box 56193
Little Rock AR 72215

www.thebutterflytypeface.com

Dedication

This book is dedicated to the greatest talents who mentored Andrew Scott Potter about Ketu Candomblé, the late icon Bira Reis from Pelourinho, Salvador, the city within a city. I give thanks to Bons Ritmos Records and Production Company and Andrew Scott Potter, my mentor, for allowing me to tell this story and share this learning experience.

I would like to give a huge shout out to Edileuza Machado and Jack Joao Potter who are very close to my heart, all inspirational for this work. Finally, to all the jazz lovers, to Black culture, to Afro Brazilian music and dance or even to shaking a tail feather, this is for you. Continue to listen to the music.

"IT'S HARD TO BE A PROFESSIONAL MUSICIAN ON DRUMS AND NOT PLAY BACKBEAT CULTURE, ROCK, RHYTHM AND BLUES, FUNK, BLUES, HIP HOP, DISCO, ELECTRONIC DANCE MUSIC, ETC. ALL USE BACK BEAT CULTURE. I'M USING THE EXACT STICKING OF THE "PI" AND "LE" PATTERNS WITH BELL SOMETIMES ON FOOT OR RIDE, AND JUST APPLYING BACKBEAT AND IT WORKS LIKE A CHARM."

~ANDREW SCOTT POTTER

Table of Contents

Introduction....................17

Chapter One:....................21

Jacks Joao Potter's Testimony....................21

Chapter Two:....................27

OPANIJE....................27

Chapter Three:....................33

ILU....................33

Chapter Four:....................37

BRAVUM....................37

Chapter Five:....................41

JINKA/ SATO....................41

Chapter Six:....................45

AVAMUNHA....................45

Chapter Seven:....................51

BATA....................51

Chapter Eight:....................53

VASSI....................53

Chapter Nine: 57

AGUERE 57

Andrew Scott Potter 61

Biography 61

Conclusion 69

Andrew Scott Potter's Message 69

About the Author 75

Jamilla Counts 75

Photo Gallery 79

References 97

Foreword

I've been commissioned by Bons Ritmos Records and Production Company to write about my learning experience while watching a series of virtual performances by Andrew Scott Potter called "JAZKET." They are filled with the discoveries by this amazing drummer who at the age of nineteen was mentored by my biological grandfather, Maulawi Nururdin, in the basement of my childhood home during the '70s alongside other great musicians.

My interest is getting these concepts of "Ketu Candomblé Codes" that have three instruments which are Rum, Pi Le, and Bell, or a Gogo/Gan. This is a story that has never been talked about or explored in jazz education or the, "jazz world" publicly.

This is territory no one has addresses before to this degree. It is my honor to reintroduce these incredible hook ups with an Afro Brazilian religion expression of rhythm and dance. Our dance styles are a sign of expression that have always been an integral part of this drum culture. We make many moves like *Cake Walk, The Black Bottom, Charlestown, Lindy Hop, Tap Dancing, Bopping, Step Dancing, Hully Gully, Boogaloo, Twist, Watutsi, Mashed Potato, Jerk, Twine, Funky Chicken, Locking, Popping, Break, Hustle*, etc. just to name a few. All of these are important to Black American culture as is reminding the world of these important innovations of jazz masters in the evolution of jazz making.

This body of work was written by a non-musician (Jamilla), for non-musicians about the untold incredible story of powerful cultural development in both countries directly related to the people brought over from West Africa. For decades, we have heard about the African Tribes being taken in Atlantic Trade, mainly to the Americas. We need to understand why the culture was banned in America, how the Black church incorporated possession into its ceremonies and how the gods were hidden behind Catholic saints in Cuba, Brazil and Haiti.

This is not another book about slavery, even though it is very relevant then and now. It's not a book rehashing the same things everyone has already written about like lynching, rape, Black Wall Street, or the Draft Riots in New York. This is about something never written about before; this book is based on Andrew's unbelievable discoveries learning the "Ketu Candomblé Codes in Jazz History" with the desire to play Brazilian rhythms better.

The book is full of information for everyone who has any interest in learning some of the fundamental elements that make up our jazz history from the past to the future. This is an extremely compact and concise look at the parallel evolution of the Ketu Candomblé Codes, one of many Afro Brazilian religions developed by the people brought to Brazil from West Africa. They were trying desperately to retain their religion and the evolution of groove phrases in solos and compositions of the great master's in jazz.

-Jamilla Counts

Acknowledgments

Andrew Scott Potter acknowledges every professional job he has done as a musician and producer, playing all kinds of musical styles which gave him the insight of the fundamentals for making music. In the visceral and in the moment, whether bandstand or recording experience, he can understand what makes each musical expression work, how he realized why he has a personal preference for certain musical expressions over others, and how certain musical expressions are made for turning off the thinking brain and getting in touch with intuition and subconscious.

Andrew would like to acknowledge the incredibly powerful and beautiful cultures of Brazil and America, their rich evolutions, traditions, dances, beats, expressions, and the inspiration from these cultures that keep him in a never-ending journey to find new discoveries about making and expressing music.

Introduction

Never in a million years could I imagine that my first book, "*A Counts Duty Assembling the Pieces of Me,*" would open Pandora box leading to some new discoveries about my family lineage. The things I've come to learn will have you flabbergasted. I was contacted by Andrew Scott Potter, who had met my mother at rehearsals with my biological grandfather Maulawi Nururdin. He always wondered what happened to her, saw the book on a Google search, and preceded to reach out to me. Starting out on bongos and congas, he would become a great drum set player. Maulawi mentored and recorded his Street Rap eclectic album released in 1974, just one year after I was born.

Through Andrew, I began to learn there is a tremendous quality of vitality and strength in these ancient West African drum dance concepts. They are interrelated, and because of the nature of the flow, if you add a beat, play it faster, and isolate the opposite hand in foundation beats, you change the character of the cadence which becomes a new approach, a new dance, a new groove, or a new style.

This is very powerful for the evolution and long-lasting power of these concepts. In the face of huge repression, these concepts arrived in each country that brought slaves to the Americas and dominated the popular musical expressions of how each perspective country expresses rhythm, groove, dancing, and singing.

This is one of the most powerful testimonies that these ancient African concepts have come to us in the present and are driving the beats and dances of right now into the future. For example," I've Got the Feeling " and " Feel It" are expressions in Black American music that allude to turning off the thinking brain and entering a space of allowing the music to direct your movement even if it's just tapping your toe to the beat.

It's important to understand how ancient African drum dance concepts have properties based on repeated polyrhythmic call response cadences with syncopation can open doors in a unique way to allow intuition, subconscious, and feeling a groove can be called "swing." In Brazil, it’s called "ginga" and basically turns off the thinking brain to be in touch with a part of us that reacts quicker than the thinking brain.

These drum dance concepts have a tremendous power to cleanse the being and center the body and soul. It cannot be underestimated that the people brought from Africa in slavery, despite repression and banning the drumming, were central to the culture and gained the strength to overcome the dehumanizing cruelty of slavery by practicing their culture clandestinely.

Chapter One:

Jacks Joao Potter's Testimony

In order for me to tell this story myself and to share it with the world, it was a must that I learn what these codes mean and understand the sound I heard. When I heard it for myself and was introduced to the culture that practices them, I had many questions.

Jack, I could relate to more, but the following interview will help you learn more about Ketu Candomblé.

Author: *What are the various Candomblé groups in Bahia?*

Jacks Joao Potter:

- Ketu Candomblé
- Angola
- Voudun
- Bantu
- Jejinago

Author: *What are some of the biggest Terreiros, the place of the ceremonies of Ketu Candomblé in Salvador?*

Jacks Joao Potter:

- Gantois
- Ileopoafonga
- Ileoxumare
- Casa Blanca

There are many other Terreiros of Candomblé of Ketu and many other Terreiros for the other sects of

Candomblé in Salvador. There are as many as there are days in the year.

Author: *Talk about the story of slave owners mixing enemy tribes.*

Jacks Joao Potter:

Pierre Verger, French author, and photographer who lived in West Africa and Salvador Bahia, in his book, "Fluxo e Refluxo," tells the story of slave owners mixing enemy tribes so they wouldn't unify and revolt. This meant Ketu Candomblé would incorporate various gods/Orixais that represented different tribes. Every Ketu Candomblé beat, which is for an Orixai (deity in the religion), has its groove. The bell actually is the center, with two drums fortifying it, and a Rum drum as solo playing set phrases with individual expression and dancers. It is a groove that starts from the beginning and up to the end.

Ketu Candomblé was codified in the mid-1800s in Brazil, when many slaves were shipped from Benin and brought their Yoroba religious ceremonies with them. Other slaves from other tribes joined in which included more Orixais and beats. Ketu Candomblé is not in every aspect of jazz, but huge chunks line up. Jazz innovators didn't know about Ketu Candomblé. They were parallel evolutions.

Where Ketu Candomblé starts a groove and holds the parts from beginning to end, jazz will use concepts mishmash.

There are three drums called "atabaques," the solo drum, the Rum, then two drums, the Pi, Rumpi and Le. They play the same rhythm, and many times, the bell or gan plays the same patterns. Therefore, this is the perfect example of how to create a "groove" or "swing." In Brazil, it's called " ginga." It's like a jazz quartet with the rhythm section holding down the swing, foundation, and chord progression while a person solos on top. Any jazz record of Miles Davis playing with John Coltrane is modal bop, and that is one of the closer approximations of American music with Ketu Candomblé concepts.

If they hadn't gone free, the harmonies and structures were simplified (yet more complex but less dense) for more expression and polyrhythms from the drums with deeper groove from everyone else.

The Ketu Candomblé drummers play a specific rhythm for the dancers. The rhythm is related to a specific Orixais, who has the ability to possess the dancer. These religions used the natural principles of ancient African drum dance concepts that were used for all aspects of life, that were made to get in touch with intuition and subconscious feeling, and that super imposed religious stories and morality for ceremonies. The feeling properties were already there in the music concepts.

Ketu Candomblé is valuable because it is frozen in time by people looking back to preserve religion. It makes it easy to study the musical principles they used trying to recreate the homeland religion. What they have in common with Black American culture is that both are preserving their culture and trying to survive in the Americas during slavery. Many times, the culture was banned.

Chapter Two:

OPANIJE

Opanije Candomblé has one of the most popular grooves around. Andrew Scott Potter expresses that I can be presented in bodily movements or by oral phases. The most important part of feeling the rhythms of dance and music is a way to feel the power of culture.

When you hear these grooves used by the late Ray Charles in the fifties, you would understand the message he was sharing in his performance like his song, "Georgia on My Mind." He was born in Albany, GA. He refused to perform in front of a segregated (all white) audience back in 1961. When he hit those keys on the piano during his performance, you could hear the frustration in his music coming out in Opanije form making the people jumping out their seats wanting to dance and storm the stage. Jamie Foxx (Collateral) stars as "Ray," giving us a look into the life of this triumphant and remarkable story of one of America's musical geniuses.

I recall my mother being one of the best dancers in the world to me. One moment in time we did " The Hokey Pokey" while preparing dinner in the kitchen. Her childhood was filled with the sound of music as was mine. Her biological father, Maulawi Nururdin, would play Milestones at Kingston Mines with Andrew Scott Potter. Only when Andrew played Ketu Candomble did he realize the hookup with the rhythm

Opanije and the A section of Milestones by Miles Davis.

Though it was super-fast on the Jazket YouTube, I could appreciate it more. Bringing down the house on the southside of Chicago at a club, Maulawi counted out the fastest tempos digging his heel into the ground of the basement apartment of Maryam and Ahmad Jamal during practice in my childhood home located at 7922 Merrill Street.

These were songs played in my childhood home. It was a very funky feel unlike some beats people can't recognize today. These beats would hit you like thunder. Louis Armstrong's "Hot Fives" is considered historic, and he uses the Opanije Candomblé cadence in a lot of his "Hot Five" solos. How these beats are similar but from radically different cultures is truly amazing. Andrew Scott Potter seems to feel that three of the best musicians: Jelly Roll Morton, Professor Longhair, and Dr. John all have a stylistic connection with a New Orleans piano tradition and the OPANIJE cadence in their music.

One of my favorite composers is Arthur Tatum Jr. who was an American jazz pianist known by other musicians as extraordinary. Many pianists attempted to copy him like my legally adopted grandfather, Ahmad Jamal. Tatum extended the vocabulary and boundaries of jazz using phrases occasionally with the OPANIJE cadence.

Andrew Scott Potter reminds us about the great James Price Johnson whose artistry would use phrases occasionally with the OPANIJE cadence but fast. This great composer's artistry was sometimes overlooked as being referred to by musicologist David Schiff as the "The Invisible Pianist" who was a major influence on other jazz musicians like Fats Waller, one of his students.

Bira Reis reminds us in his YouTube that the drums call the Orixais. The party for the Orixais doesn't start without the drums. The Rum player who plays solos and the deeper drum with one hand and one stick, has set combinations that communicate with the Orixais and that also make the dancer do specific moves. The techniques evolved over time. The drummers would start filling in more spaces with flans and "ruffs."

You don't have to be a drum player to understand the groove.

Chapter Three:
ILU

Andrew Scott Potter states that ILU is a very powerful rhythm used in dance located in Brazil, like Coco, Pifinu, Forro, Baiao, and more. It can be found in our most popular rhythms and dances today to which most people are not paying attention. Andrew is barely scratching the surface performing these great beats on his drums, ILU is a massively powerful groove, and it contains a lot of secrets and codes that are in Black American musical history and evolution which has been part of most all-American popular music. Not saying these new groups study the Ketu religion but they seem to share a similar cultural origin.

By playing it at all tempos, slowing it down, leading with the opposite hand, and putting a back beat on it, it really is a tremendous force," as he bangs with great force. His red hair blows in the air as his head moves back and forth. I'm feeling the music.

I noticed that even though Andrew doesn't practice the Candomblé religion himself, he shows his respect by wearing a nice red bracelet around his neck while performing on one of his YouTube channels. It was a gift from his brother who went to Kenya, and the necklaces were made for him by his son.

The great Scott Joplin (piano), known to the world as, "The King of Ragtime" from his Pulitzer winning opera to rag inspired classical waltz. His collection is filled with complex bass patterns that are still imitated by composers today. As one of the landmark American composers of the 20th century, many of his songs were filled with these KETU Candomblé codes. Many people know him from the song "The Entertainer," and from the movie *The Sting* with Paul Newman and Robert Redford. "The Entertainer" has lots of ILU cadences. Looking back on some of the old dances, "The Charleston" is very much in the Ketu Candomblé cadence.

I always have claimed that my mother has been my guarding angel all my life. There is a song that I've always adored from the very first time I heard it. Now, I could have mixed emotions when looking back on my mother's murder. "On the Wings of Love" (has the ILU rhythm) was written by Jeffrey Osborne from his self-titled debut album released in 1982. It was written alongside Peter Schless; the song was the second single from the album. In my mind, when I would hear this song, it gave me comfort that my mother (my angel) was watching over me.

In this generation, we all enjoy Bruno Mars, known for his stage performances and his swag style

performing in a wide range of musical styles including pop, reggae, disco, soul, and rock. Mars is accompanied by his band, "The Hooligans," who play a variety of instruments such as electric guitar, bass, piano, keyboard, drums, and horns. They also serve as backup singers and dancers always playing slick good music to get the girls. In one of his greatest hits, "Leave the Door Open," you can hear three sections. Section A is a slow ILU, even the kicks fall in. There is a transition B section into a C section hook/chorus that seems to fall with OPANIJE.
That is the thing about mishmash, you can have one groove that can imply one thing and another at the same time like BRAVUM swing with soloist phrasing OPANIJE.
Especially in pop, rhythm and blues, and soul music, it can change the beat when there is a key change modulation in the arrangement, a B section for example. Older jazz, swing, disco, and hip hop don't often change the beat on their modulations. Later, jazz would do that. My biological grandfather, Maulawi, did it in his writing as well.

Chapter Four:
BRAVUM

BRAVUM is all about that bounce swing that European notation can't write accurately, but you can feel in those hips or buttocks when you hear the music playing (Ha ha!).

That's the humor in me.

While defining what this code means, Andrew brings a question to mind. How do you define swing in jazz? Do they teach you what swing is in the academy? European notation can't really do it justice because they make it either triplet or dotted.

But all instrumentalists, when they read jazz notation and see eight note runs, know they have to "swing" it.

Being raised in Memphis, I'm surrounded by blues and rock. In 1903, the city became the home of musicians who created the "Blues on Beale Street" after Major Thornton contacted a trumpet player out of Clarksdale, Mississippi named W.C. Handy.

When you are not singing the blues downtown, you can ride over to Graceland in the Whitehaven neighborhood, south of Central, just a few miles north of the Mississippi borders to catch a feel of Elvis Aaron Presley, the "King of Rock and Roll" and one of the most significant cultural figures of the 20th century.

Andrew brought to our attention to a few things. "Count Basie was noted as one of the hardest swinging big bands in the era, and his players innovated aspects of the swing era like Papa Jo Jones, who put the *splang a lang* (opposite hand in the "pi" and "le" in BRAVUM) up in a raised ride cymbal," but after the GoGo sound came to New York from artists like Chuck Brown, the one group he mentioned that hit home for me and that used these beats was a hip new bouncy sound that came up to New York and created a whole new groove. Jack Swing became a worldwide dance created by Kid'n Play.

The world would catch on to this amazing group watching the comedy film called *House Party*, directed by Reginald Hiding in 1990. This was during a time in my life when I was living on the southside of Chicago and where the houses in my hood stayed filled with block parties. Chuck Brown and the Gogo scene came to New York and influenced Kid'n Play.

During my research, I was amazed to find that the drummer for Elvis Presley in the early songs, DJ

Fontana, used a BRAVUM cadence in the ride cymbal many times. Those were some memorable days when I visited Graceland for the very first time. It is such big a place that you have to visit more than once to see everything.

Charlie Parker was one of the most brilliant American musicians from the bebop era, and his classic bebop standard would get his own movie!

Charlie "Yardbird" Parker was a pioneer of bebop with his incredible and complex saxophone solos. The great actor and director, Clint Eastwood, stepped away from the Wild West to explore jazz, one of his other passions, in this moody 1988 biopic movie called, *Bird* played by Forest Whitaker. He wrote this great hit called, "Now's the Time," which has various phrases that fall right into BRAVUM/JINKA bell pattern.

Chapter Five:

JINKA/ SATO

JINKA is another incredible rhythm that addresses a bouncy feeling relating to swing in jazz in a big way. Keep in mind that, "It actually shares the exact same bell part as BRAVUM and the exact same " pi" and " le" as SATO. Many blues players like BB King from

Memphis, TN and jazz piano players in the swing era would use a lick that sounded like "tata Diggity /tata Diggity," in their solos, and that is right out the JINKA cadence.

For example, I'm sure we are all familiar with the song, "Jingle Bell, Jingle Bell, Jingle Rock." The phrase has the exact pattern of JINKA BRAVUM bell part. In my opinion, you can't celebrate the Christmas Holidays without grooving or singing this song at least once.

One great musician we all miss is Duke Ellington who wrote "Satin Doll." This great jazz standard was written in 1953; it seems to catch accents in the JINKA bounce. It's been said by his father, Mercer Ellington, that "Satin Doll" was written for Duke's longtime mistress Bea "Evie" Ellis. It is some of the best music created from the heart that has a beat.

On the other hand, SATO has one extra beat in the bell part of BRAVUM and JINKA, to make it triple meter (3/4 in European notation) and uses the exact same "pi" and "le" as JINKA. SATO plays the same thing, but the one extra beat on the bell, makes it triple meter or 3/4. Jinka has the same bell part as Bravum which is related to that bouncy feeling in the jazz, swing, and bebop. It has modal jazz periods and a different accent. You can find it in the way Ellington writes some syncopations over swing.

You can find it in the way Elvin took it from "*splang a lang*" to "*splang a langity.*" It's got that difference from Bravum.

Andrew states that it's important to remember, "Part of the vitality, strength, and survival of these ancient African concepts that come all the way down to us today, in popular cultures, throughout the Americas, is this dynamic that slight changes make it something fresh and new; because you change one beat, it becomes something else, a new style, a new dance."

John Coltrane would take standards like "My Favorite Things" and play syncopations that link it with SATO from my understanding.

Chapter Six:
AVAMUNHA

AVAMUNHA is a driven-on top of the beat groove. I have come to learn that, "singing and dancing enable the embodiment of the 'emotional essence'" (MERLEAU-PONTY, 1945) of Candomblé, whereas their intellectual and semantic understanding as well as their technical precision become secondary. For the primacy of the religion lies on the bodily experience and sharing of this very essence both with the community and with the gods, the orixás." Upon listening to the sound, there is a 3/2, like Cuban Clave, in the bell, but the "pi" and "le" have a groove where the opposite hand is laying down an anticipation. This explains many approaches in solos by instrument who start throwing out an accent that is anticipated every beat, pushing the momentum on the beat.

Dizzy Gillespie is an icon of the bebop era, and some of his compositions would use an AVAMUNHA, anticipated edge in the lines. He was a great jazz trumpeter, bandleader, composer, educator, and singer. As a great trumpet virtuoso and improviser, he was known for building on the virtuosic style of Roy Eldridge while adding layers of rhythmic complexity previously unheard in jazz in the 1940's. He would write sharp anticipating lines for an edge effect that approximates the opposite hand in the Pi and Le of AVAMUNHA.

In jazz, you can find it in compositions, and a soloist can use it as an accent in the solo. In Samba, this anticipation-type attack you find in AVAMUNHA can be used by soloists with anticipation in the attack of the piano.

Many of my ancestors migrated from Cuba. I've never been to this part of the world, but it sounds like an exciting place to visit one day.

I was very saddened to see in the news this week that Irene Cara passed away due to reasons unknown. An American singer, songwriter, and actress, Cara rose to prominence for her role as Coco Hernandez in the 1980 musical film *Fame*/recording the film's title song "Fame," reached No. 1 in several countries.

In 1983, Cara sang and co-wrote the song, " Flashdance...What a Feeling," which won a Grammy Award for Best Female Pop Vocal Performance in 1984. I'm awestruck to discover from Andrew Scott Potter, himself, that he had the privilege to work with her as a dance accompanist for the choreography of

Fame. Another spectacular talent who choreographed the "Kiss" video by Prince was Louis Falco. What a dancer!

He crossed her path when she came into the dance auditions at Louis Falco studio. She had already been cast as Coco. She said she played congas and percussion. He handed her some bongos, and they were jamming out.

Andrew went to record a part they filmed but later cut, and Irene was there recording, "Out Here on My Own." She had one of the most beautiful voices he recalls. He worked with Minnie Ripperton and Jingle singers in Chicago. He knew right then what really good singing sounded like.

What a talent!

In disco, electric dance music, and hip hop, you can find many Ketu Candomblé codes layered over each other.

Disco used to be recorded with live musicians including one of New York's top musicians, Steve

Gadd. The "and 1 and 2 and 3 and 4 and" of the hi-hat anticipating the beat and the four bass drumbeats to the bar, approximates the anticipation of the foundation beats in AVAMUNHA. Hip hop, which innovated whole new beat approaches, broke up the beats a lot, and you can find ILU and OPANIJE among other Ketu Candomblé cadences or phrases, even in some rap phrasing. Even in dance music without direct hi-hat, anticipation is still implied. "Fame" and "Flashdance" implicate a driving anticipation anchored by a bass drum hard on the one, centering it like a disco beat. Electronic dance music is generated by the computer but anchored on top of the ancient African drum dance concepts with Ketu Candomblé cadences as well.

Chapter Seven:
BATA

BATA is a slower lilting beat; amazingly, it can fit with most standard jazz ballads as well as some styles of slow rhythms and blues. It speaks to the fact that a good jazz ballad has to have some kind of swing to it even at its most ethereal. "Blue in Green" on the

Miles Davis record "Kind of Blue," could be done with the BATA rhythm over it.

A pop rhythm and blues song by the Flamingos, "I Only Have Eyes for You," fits very well with the BATA beat.

Theodore DeReese Pendergrass (Teddy) was born in Kingstree, South Carolina. Pendergrass spent most of his life in the Philadelphia area and initially rose to musical fame as the lead singer of Harold Melvin & the Blue Notes.

Landing a solo career in 1976, Pendergrass capitalized on his baritone lothario image, most notably with his trademark "ladies only" concerts. He scored hits with the single "I Don't Love You Anymore," one of my favorite go-to songs that has BATA rhythm.

Fans were devastated when, at age 31, he was critically injured after his Rolls-Royce hit a tree. I was one of those fans who was devastated to hear of his accident leaving him in a wheelchair.

Still, it didn't stop him from singing.

Chapter Eight:

VASSI

VASSI is a powerful rhythm; it's done at various tempos in Ketu Candomblé for various orixais. It actually could fit with all swing beats in jazz songs. It is just that BRAVUM has the actual swing slang a lang in it, but VASSI has many properties that would fit over swing and is used in solo energies by many players and compositions.

I've come to learn that "A slow swing by John Coltrane, Equinox has a cadence that VASSI implicates." As many times as I've listened to "Footprints" by Wayne Shorter, I now realize that he used a feeling that goes with VASSI very well." I never could relate to his style of jazz.

In the late fifties and early sixties, while many jazz musicians began abandoning the ancient African polyrhythmic, repeated bars, simple forms, for odd times, complex arrangements and forms, and linear concepts etc.

Various high-level jazz musicians were going deeper into the ancient African concepts by simplifying the forms for more expression and polyrhythms, cutting edge 20th century Western European Harmony, and more songs in 6/8 time like the Cuban Congueiro (Cuba is also a powerhouse culture with huge ties to ancient African concepts). Mongo Santamaria writing

Afro Blue was done by many jazz musicians including John Coltrane.

This was the Hard Bop, Modal Bop style, still using 12-bar blues structures and AABA 32-bar forms, but introducing more Cuban clave, 6/8 and 3/4 times using simple forms for deeper improvisation and feeling.

Chapter Nine:
AGUERE

AGUERE is a beat that you can find in American music from Scott Joplin to pop music and is very much like a Calypso beat that has a distinctive feature in music. A syncopated rhythm "offbeat" pattern, often three-beat rhythms with two long beats followed by a short beat. Calypso music is, "a type of folk song primarily from Trinidad though sung elsewhere in the southern and eastern Caribbean islands.

The subject of a calypso text, usually witty and satiric, is a local and topical event of political and social import, and the tone is one of illusion, mockery, and double entendre." The pattern goes down, down, up.... up, down, up. That seems to be the strumming pattern. You start with a down strum using your index finger; then, follow it with another down stroke using your thumb. It includes a style/rhythm of four on the floor with the feel of just the kick, the snare is playing the 8th note before every other kick, and the quarter note is between the others.

Along with Andrew, I believe the song "Hey Leroy, Your Mama's Calling You" by Jimmy Walter Castor was a big hit in 1966. He was an American funk, R&B, and soul musician. He is credited with vocals, saxophone, and composition. He is best known for songs such as "It's Just Begun," "The Bertha Butt Boogie," and his biggest hit single, the million-seller "Troglodyte (Cave Man). Castor was once described as "one of the most sampled artists in music history" by the British Broadcasting Corporation (BBC). His music for sure had Cuban clave roots, but AGUERE from Ketu, fit like a charm.

Ralph MacDonald, a Grammy Award-winning percussionist and composer is known as "The Ghost" behind the hit records of a multitude of 1970s and 1980s pop stars. He had a hit in the '80s with a powerful Calypso flavor. AGUERE also approximates the groove feeling.

Ralph MacDonald, who was a co-writer of the hit songs "Where Is the Love?" and "Just the Two of Us," died in Stamford, Conn. at 67 years old. His bio page tells the story of seventeen-year-old, Ralph, "who helped a friend carry his steel drums into an audition for legendary performer Harry Belafonte. The friend got the gig, and MacDonald became a regular at rehearsals.

When one of the players in Belafonte's Steel Band was late for a rehearsal, Ralph brashly declared his ability to play and wound up getting the job. Thus began a 10-year stint with Belafonte that schooled

MacDonald in the music business. It also introduced him to the songwriter, Bill Salter, and the two began writing together to fill time on the road. At one-point, young MacDonald had the nerve to tell Harry Belafonte that despite all the gold records on the wall, Belafonte didn't really know what Calypso was.

As he became well-known in the music industry, popular artists wanted his services, and he increasingly worked in the styles of pop, easy listening, and light music in general.

Who doesn't remember his disco was at its peak in 1977 when the movie *Saturday Night Fever* came out?

Three songs by The Bee Gees spent a total of 15 weeks at the top of the Hot 100 Billboard chart. The world watched John Travolta wearing that same white suit the group wore on the cover of their album.

The music just made you groove no matter what was going on in your life.

Andrew Scott Potter

Biography

Andrew Scott Potter was mentored about Ketu Candomblé, by the late Bira Reis. They both performed, in Pelorinho, right in front of Bira's incredible culture store. Andrew has recorded with various artists. He co-founded Bons Ritmos Records in 1986 and released 16 CDs including two Billboard

World Music charting CDs by Edi Machado that received over 200 radio stations playing cuts from the CDs. He also co-produced four CDs of the Rio de Janeiro Jazz Trio on Mix House Label with Paulo Russo. He has backed the expert Afro-Bahian dancer on video and tours throughout Brazil and the U.S. He performed with Gabi Guedes, master Candomblé drummer, at Ivan Huel's Jam no Mam in Salvador with special guest sax player, Marcelo Martins, doing Ketu Candomblé rhythms to Wayne Shorter compositions. He has worked with various Rainha de Carnival passistas including Marja Nunes, Lydia, Paola, and Alexandra. He recorded in the studio in Bahia with master Ketu Candomblé drummer Bira Sanros, Gilmareo Marquis, Maestro Memeu, Katatau, etc.

Born in Chicago, Andrew worked professionally with Maulawi. He recorded his first sideman record with Rufus Reid on bass, and he worked for Bunky Green, Bill Brimfield, Fred Anderson, Odell Brown, the Organisers (who used Andrew on the first leg of the Perfect Angel release tour with Minnie Ripperton) Ken

Prince, Fred Hopkins, Cleveland Eaton, George Hunter big band (with sometimes sidemen Muhal Richard Abrams, Thurman Barker, Frank Gordon, and Pete Cosey). He worked at the Four Seasons restaurant with Richard Evans and Larry Grey. His first co-record release was with Eric Hochberg and David E. Tillman, who had released two records as co-leader when he was in New York, that were picked up twice by other labels.

Other people he worked with were Steve Rodby, John Campell, Kestutis Stanciauskas with whom he recorded several records, the group Streetdancer with Chico Freeman, Ari Brown, Steve Eisen, Bob Long, and other Chicago musicians. Later, he would tour the Kaunus Jazz Fest with Streetdancer.

He broke Henry Johnson in Chicago at the Bulls, John Marsh, Billy Dickens, Richard Smith, Jerome Cooper, Rollo Radford, Steve McCall, Brad Bobo, and Robert Shy. He worked in the Free Street Theater for one year with Katharine Dunham and Wilbert Bradley doing Afro-diasporic dances.

Andrew moved to New York in 1978. His first job was for Alex Foster and Michael Wolff with sidemen Jimmy Ponder, John Scofield, Lincoln Goines, Chip Jackson, Dave Saltman, and other great musicians. He then worked at the Harlem club, Club Wells, for Walter Bishop Jr. with Marcus Miller, Carmen Lundy, Ricky Ford (who did a tenor battle for Walter Bishop Jr. with Dave Shnitter and Ford at Seventh Ave South), and Potter and Marcus Miller. He toured Bermuda and the Bahamas on the Jazz Cruz for Walter Bishop Jr. and Cecilia Payne with John Ore on bass.

He played with Ryo Kawasaki, Clint Houston, Russel Blake, and Tony Cimorosi who had Steve Grossman on a job with Bruce Whitcomb and Potter. He played in New York and toured Paris, Metz, and Geneva, Switzerland with Sonny Sharrok. Andrew played clubs in Harlem with Dr. Lonnie Smith and Richie Hart. He recorded two records for Nannette Natel and performed shows with her, Walter Bishop Jr., Rufus Reid, Tony Cimorosi, Todd Coolman, and Dave Gordon. He recorded "Justo Almario" and his "Potter Tillman: Coasting" release.

He did an Ellen Burstyn production of Shakespeare's *A Midsummer Night's Dream* with Christopher Waken as well as an off-Broadway production of *They Were All Gardenias* with Walter Bishop Jr. and Carmen Lundy.

Andrew worked extensively in New York in the dance world. He worked on the movie *Fame* for choreographer Louis Falco during rehearsal for the dancers including Irene Cara and Neisha Folkes (future Alvin Ailey dancer who did a video clip for Potter). He was the music director for Sal Perneice for several seasons. He played during dance class for various dance performers including Jenifer Muller, Clay Talifaro, Bill Gornell, Lisa Nalven, and many more. He toured Hamburg, Germany with Gail Conrad Tap CO.

In 1986, he moved to Rio de Janeiro for a journey to Brazil from which he would never look back. He played with trumpeter Barrosinho, founder of Banda Black Rio. On the jobs with him were the top musicians of Rio. Samba bass innovator, Luizao Maia, recorded for Andrew's Bons Ritmos label later. Paulo Russo, one of the top acoustic bass players anywhere, became co-leader of the Rio de Janeiro Jazz Trio that released four records on Mix House.

Paulo brought in legends for Bons Ritmos projects like Gilson Peranzzetta, Luiz Avelar, Kiko Continentino, Rafael Vernet, João Rebouces, Marcelo Martins, and Idris Boudriouar. They participated in the Porto das Galinhas Jazz Fest and played clubs in Recife. He produced the Mini Jazz Fest at Pedra de Toque in Recife and the Rio das Ostras Jazz Fest in the state of Rio de Janeiro.

Andrew hired the BBC winner of the singer of the millennium of Brazil, Elza Soares, to participate on the first Billboard charting CD of Edi Machado. They made a video with her also.

Andrew lived briefly in Recife Pernambuco, where he was very affected by the powerful culture there and played and recorded with various top level musicians. Ranieri Ricardo Oliveira now writes music for novellas on TV Recorde including Gustavo Anacleto, Fabinho Costa, Renato Bandeira, Euclides, Braulio Araujo, and Beenardo Jose of Nacao Pernambuco. Andrew was honored to play with Coco groups: Coco Raizes do Arco Verde, and the late Aurinha de Coco.

Thanks to his son, he performed in Salvador with musicians from Olodum, Maestro Memeo, Gilmario Marques, Andre Silva, Katatau, and more and recorded them on a record "Movimento Percusivo."

Conclusion

Andrew Scott Potter's Message

This is the message that Andrew Scott Potter wants to convey to the world, "Ketu Candomblé, for us in America, is a signpost not only to the ancient African origins, but it speaks to how people brought from Africa in the slave trade to America were the same as those brought to Brazil. We can understand our (yes, that can mean Black Americans, but in truth, it's the cultural road map of American culture that all Americans should know and embrace) cultural origins on a much higher level of understanding."

My search for my roots brought a greater understanding of myself. This is the same on a collective level that Black Americans do have roots and origins they can discover, and it can bring a greater understanding of the contributions and force of these ancient African concepts. We have to know "Africa" is way too big and complex with way too many ethnicities to do justice to the people brought to the Americas.

It's like thinking South America describes Brazil; it absolutely does not. We are talking about ancient traditional mostly West African tribes and cultures and their cultures to get this. For example, the IGBO and Bambuti Pygmies are two ancient peoples with dramatic ethnic differences who share certain rhythms and dance concepts, but they are not exactly alike.

A pharaoh in Egypt, 4000 years ago, remarked on the incredible dancing skills of his court pygmy dancers from the interior of Africa. You know these concepts were happening back then, so the big question is, "Who put two against three in a cross-rhythm as a cadence, cell, bar, or two bars in European terminology and repeated it over and over and over? These YouTube channels (educational tool) have given me the visual and desire to tap the beats I hear, to understand, and to pay attention to the origins of harmonic progressions and turning systems that once came from the basement of my childhood home mentioned in "*A Counts Duty: Assembling the Pieces of Me*."

I'm now filled with the knowledge of my biological grandfather, Maulawi Nururdin's works and the importance of their love for jazz and their contribution to jazz history. I finally began to learn the music notes. I'm cracking a smile for a moment because I am moved by a statement made by Andrew Scott Potter, "I didn't make these discoveries from an academic background, or a scholastic background, or as a teacher. I discovered their concepts as a playing musician."

Being a substitute teacher in the Benton School District from 2012 to 2020 working in music classes was initially like going to a foreign country for me.

I became even more passionate about music and jazz watching a group called The String Queens (TSQ). This dynamic trio creates stimulating musical experiences that inspire diverse audiences giving love and hope to this new generation. This group released their third album called, "RISE," which was made possible by an MPower Artist Grant from the Sphinx Organization that is filled with a multitude of musical genres.

A repertoire spanning from the Baroque Era to the Jazz Age to today's Billboard Hot 100 Chart. These wonderful three Black queens who are classroom educators surely got my attention redoing," Sometimes I Feel Like a Motherless Child," which was also done by my legally adopted grandfather Ahmad Jamal.

This group is a great example of the importance of teaching this new generation the evolution and long-lasting power of these powerful concepts that should be learned in the classroom.

In the face of huge repression, these concepts arrived in each country that brought slaves to the Americas and dominated the popular music expressions affecting how each perspective country expresses rhythm, groove, dance, and singing.

They should be a part of the school curriculum throughout our nation.

About the Author

Jamilla Counts

Jamilla Counts is back with another deep and poignant look into her past.

In her debut memoir, *A Count's Duty: Assembling the Pieces of Me*, we learn not only of the author's tragic lineage but also of her musical heritage by way of her legal adopted grandfather, Ahmad Jamal.

In her sophomore title, Counts delves deeper into her past and introduces a new friendship with Andrew Scott Potter. Potter worked and recorded for her biological grandfather, Maulawi Nururdin.

This intensely personal body of work is based on Jamilla's extensive research findings and Potter's desire to make and share music.

Black American Music Evolution: The Ketu Candomblé Codes is for those who love jazz and are interested in its evolution and history.

A single mother of two adult daughters and one granddaughter, Jamilla was born in Chicago in 1973 and partly raised on the south side in early her childhood. Her family later moved to Memphis, Tennessee to run an inherited family business.

As a rebellious child who didn't finish high school, she finally got her act together and later received her GED in 2005. She continued her education process at

Pulaski Technical College and received her associate's degree. She continued to further her education at the University of Arkansas, Little Rock in the Social Work Program while being a resident and was a former substitute teacher after eight years of working for the Benton School District. She moved back to Memphis, the place she calls home after seventeen years.

In honor of her paternal sister Airickca Gordon Taylor (cousin of Emmett Till), who passed away of March 2020 from Kidney failure and spent her life educating others about the black teenage lynching victim's legacy through her foundation, Jamilla has become an activist herself standing for the people of Memphis.

One murder victim she holds dear to her heart was killed by the hands of the police, Tyre Nichols, whose story was reported nationwide:

Protestors Block Streets for hours to demand justice for Nichols:
https://www.cbs42.com/news/protesters-block-streets-for-hours-to-demand-justice-for-nichols/

Jamilla has stood for preserving history and justice through her works. She is currently working for the Memphis Center for Health and Rehabilitation for the elderly (St. Peters Villa.) She enjoys being of service and giving back to her community. She still enjoys writing, cracking a joke or two, and spending time cultivating the lives of children.

Photo Gallery

Jack Joao Potter playing Rum atabaque with Ivan Santana from Swing de pelo at a show at Bira Reis.
(Photo by Yasmin Reis)

Andrew mentor about Ketu Candomble, Pelorinho icon,

Jack Joao Potter, Bons Ritmos artist is on the right, Bira Reis is in the middle.Katato of Olodum is on the left in a show at the stop of Bira Reis in Pelorinho, Salvador Bahia (Photo by Yasmin Reis)

The dancer is Edi Machado, two time world beat billboard chart artist in a show performed in Pelorinho, Salvador Bahia, the shop of Bira Reis. (Photo by Yasmin Reis)

Bon Ritmos, Andrew Scott Potter, Edi Machado, Jack Joao Potter at the studio of Carlinhos Brown, llha de Sapos, Candeia Salvador Bahia

Music chart of all the bell parts

Bon Ritmos Studio in Salvador
(Secrets of Ketu Candomblé Dances and Drumming)

Hot Five / Louis Armstrong

Count Basie Big Band

Jellyroll Morton

Duke Ellington

Art Tatum

John Coltrane Quartet

Miles Davis

Chuck Brown – Washington, DC GoGo Legend

(GoGo was the precursor to Jack Swing)

Charlie Parker, Dizzy Gillespie, Max Roach (Very important picture of three great innovators in jazz of the Bebop era)

Front and back covers of the Bons Ritmos release,
Jazz Standards, Afro Bahian Rhythms

Jack playing Rum Atabaque with Edi Machado,
(Photo by Yasmin Reis)

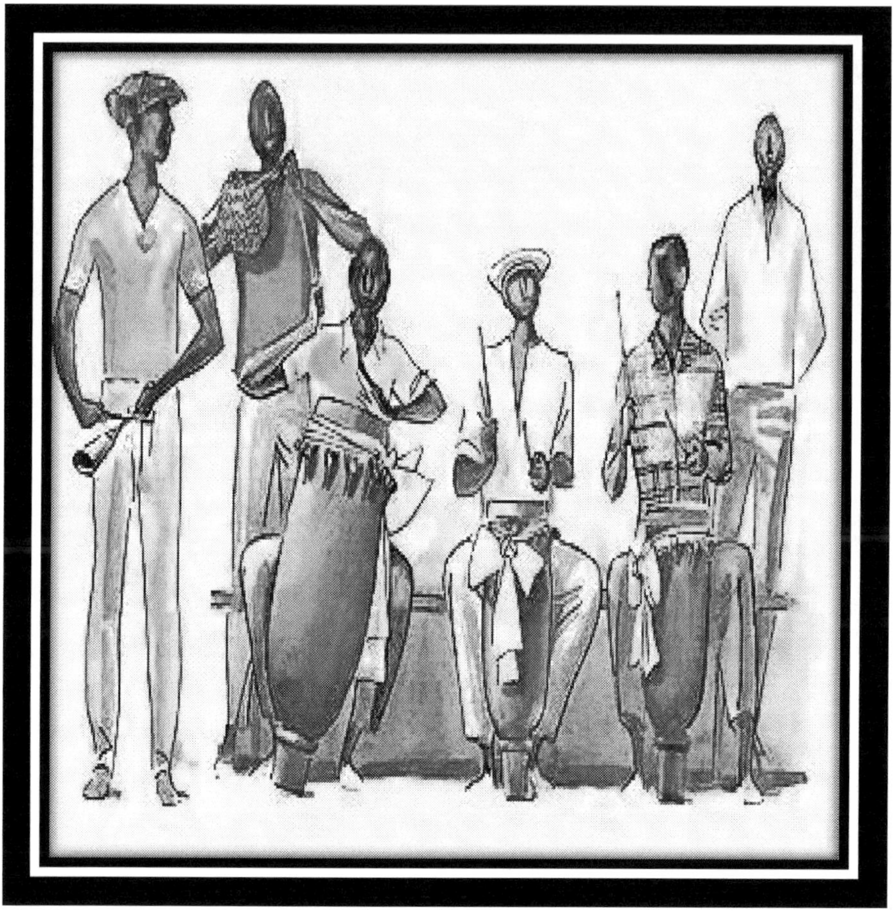

Ketu Candomble Orchestra Rum, Pi or Rumpi, Le, Gan

Elvin Jones

Gabi Guedes

Herbie Hancock

Irene Cara

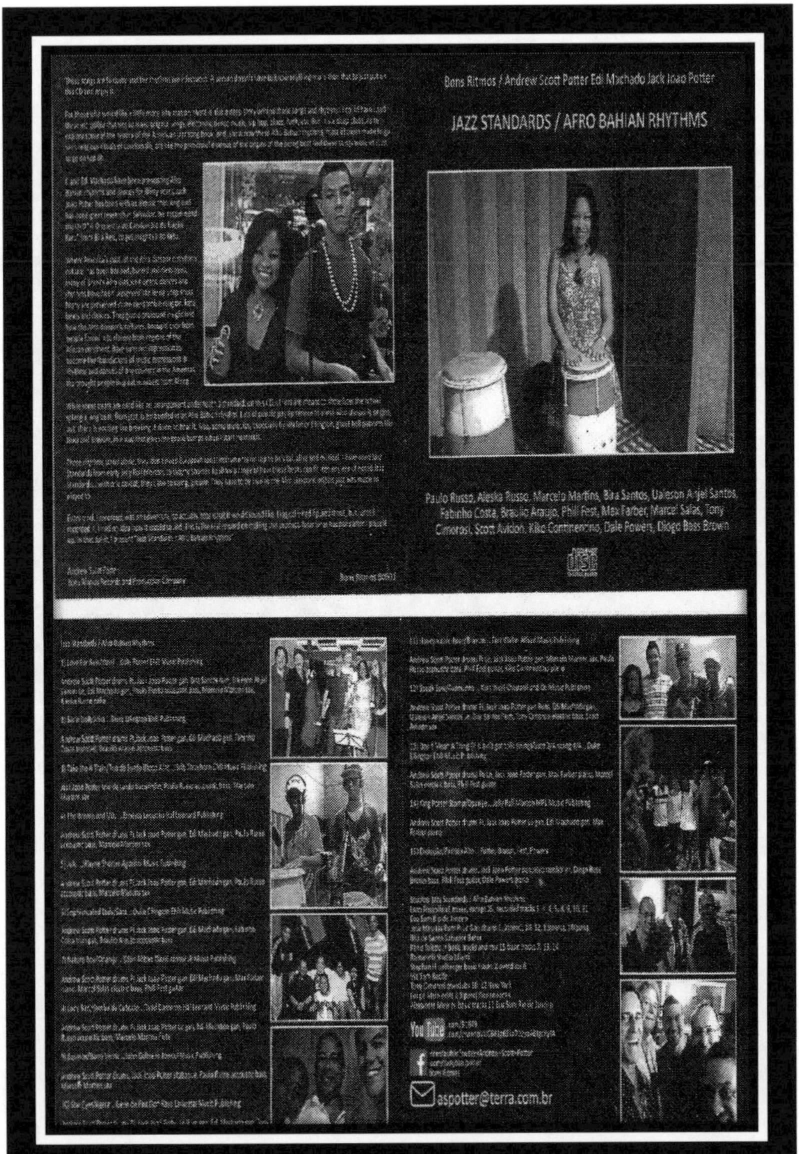

Jazz Standards Afro Bahian Rhythms

Jimmy Garrison

McCoy Tyner

Ron Carter

Scott Joplin

Wayne Shorter

Maulawi Nururdin in the basement of Chicago home (7922 Merrill Street) during author's childhood.

Maulawi Nururdin, Street Rap Album: Street Rap – YouTube:
https://youtu.be/6UkGduOR2Ko

References

AllAboutJazz
https://www.allaboutjazz.com/musicians/discography/andrew-scott-potter

Andrew Scott Potter
https://www.discogs.com/artist/2128202-Andrew-Scott-Potter

Andrew Scott Potter at 70, Milestone with F. Costa, T.Cimorosi, J.Amorim, J. Potter
https://youtu.be/HiDk5IBwuAk

Apple Music
https://music.apple.com/us/artist/andrew-scott-potter/152817324

Amazon
https://www.amazon.com/Preciosa-Andrew-Scott-Potter/dp/B000JHRL10

Bandcamp
https://erichochberg.bandcamp.com/album/future-tense-3

Bons Ritmos YouTube Channel

https://m.youtube.com/channel/UCM4qH4HR_Dsdpc45CphwUwQ/videos

"CHAPTER 2: ILU /KETU CANDOMBLÉ CODES IN JAZZ EVOLUTION HISTORY | [DFO] Drum Forum"

https://www.drumforum.org/threads/chapter-2-ilu-ketu-Candomblé-codes-in-jazz-evolution-history.171260/

Chapter 5,6,7,8: KETU Codes in JAZZ Andrew Potter Scott https://youtu.be/8zCFT3Dz-D4

Festa Yemanja dances costumes

https://m.youtube.com/watch?v=sJxNjx4aBX8&t=969s

Future Tense by Eric Hochberg, Steve Eisen, and Andrew Scott Potter

https://erichochberg.bandcamp.com/album/future-tense-3

Gabi Guedes YouTube Channel

https://m.youtube.com/c/GabiGuedesMusic

Hot House: New York's Premier Jazz Guide
[PDF] February 2021 pdf-hot house jazz
WWW.hothousejazz.com
[PDF] Hot House December.pdf
WWW.hothousejazz.com

"Incredible: Ketu Candomblé codes in jazz - Jazz Music Forum" Chapter Three

http://www.jazzmusicarchives.com/forum/forum_posts.asp?TID=26719&OB=DESC

Jack Potter YouTube Channel

https://m.youtube.com/channel/UC681g6Zka702yaABJgcXyfA/videos

JAZKET: KETU CANDOMBLÉ CODES IN JAZZ. ANDREW POTTER SCOTT all chapters combined

https://youtu.be/eo7NNuHGa_M

Jazket Hot Fives Louis Armstrong/Opanije

https://m.youtube.com/watch?v=rdlvgrjRwtI

Jazket YouTube Channel

https://m.youtube.com/channel/UClpDp25xd4RJ1t3NpVg5eLQ/videos

Jazz Archives
https://www.jazzmusicarchives.com/artist/andrew-scott-potter

Jazz Standards/Afro-Bahian Rhythms

https://m.youtube.com/watch?v=pzu6KOrvFTM&t=3555s

Jazz Times
https://jazztimes.com/artists/andrew-scott-potter/

“Ketu Candomblé origins in backbeat culture on drum set"

https://www.drumchat.com/showthread.php/38081-Ketu-Candomblé-origins-in-backbeat-culture-on-drum-set

"Listening with the Body: An Aesthetics of Spirit Possession Outside the Terreiro on JSTOR"

https://www.jstor.org/stable/10.5406/ethnomusicology.60.1.0089

"Opanije - Best Percussion Rhythms and Traditions" https://opanije.com/best-percussion-rhythms-and-traditions/

MAULAWI NURURDIN: Street Rap

https://youtu.be/6UkGduOR2Ko

Music Metason https://music.metason.net/artistinfo?name=Andrew%20Scott%20Potter

Orchestra Ketu Candomblé https://m.youtube.com/watch?v=kUgdwkBD-P8

(PDF) Candomblé Rituals and Food Practices in Italy and Brazil

https://www.academia.edu/45606478/Candombl%C3%A9_rituals_and_food_practices_in_Italy_and_Brazil_an_ethnographic_comparison

References "the secrets to swing groove in the history of jazz are here: | Sax on the Web Forum"

https://www.saxontheweb.net/threads/the-secrets-to-swing-groove-in-the-history-of-jazz-are-here.354260/

Slave Trade Video:

Top 10 African Tribes Taken In The Atlantic Slave Trade

The Hippodrome of Music: Andrew Scott Potter

https://hippodrome.net/tag/andrew-scott-potter/

The story behind Ralph Macdonald: The Music Aficionado

https://musicaficionado.blog/2018/07/31/the-artistry-of-ralph-macdonald/

Wolfgang's
https://www.wolfgangs.com/andrew-scott-potter/

BONS RITMOS RECORDS E PRODUÇÕES

Bons Ritmos Records Productions

YOUR STORY MATTERS
Butterfly Typeface Publishing

Made in the USA
Columbia, SC
16 December 2023

30c202dd-5d72-4707-b743-ab94e1247de7R01